Property of St. Luke's
Episcopal Church

248

Touched
By
God

D0048049

Parish Library
St. Luke's Episcopal Church
Prescott, AZ 86301

Parish Library
St. Luke's Episcopal Church

Touched By God

My Pilgrimage of Prayer

John Powell, S.J.

ThomasMore®

Allen, Texas

This book was originally published under the title *He Touched Me*.

Photos by Jean-Claude Lejeune

Copyright © 1974, 1996 by John Powell, S. J.

All rights reserved. No part of this book shall be reproduced or transmitted in any form or by any means, electronic or mechanical, including photocopying, recording, or by any information or retrieval system, without written permission from the Publisher:

Send all inquiries to:

Thomas More® Publishing
200 East Bethany Drive
Allen, Texas 75002-3804

Printed in the United States of America

ISBN 0–88347–328–3

14 15 16 17 18   00 99 98 97 96

Childhood: The Beginnings

After thirty years of detours and dead-end seeking, St. Augustine found, in his moment of surrender, all that had previously eluded him. "Our hearts," he said, "were made for you, O God, and they shall not rest until they rest in you." Augustine knew in the end what the poet Goethe expressed in his line: "All human longing is really longing for God." Augustine, like so many of us, lost his childhood version of faith in order to find God in a sadder but wiser middle age.

His own reflection on those lost years was this: "Too late have I loved you, O Lord, too late have I loved you. Memory is indeed a sad privilege."

Very early in life, as I now remember, this shape of the human heart, a frail vessel painfully empty until it holds God's presence, was somehow clear to me. I am sure that my child's faith was largely an echo of my mother's, but there was something else; there was the ever gentle touch of God, like a soft hand caressing the face of my soul. And there was a hunger. I used to think that, when my mother and father turned out all the lights in our house and went to bed at night, the throb of life throughout the whole world also shut down. Everybody slept at once. And so God would not be quite so busy at this time and would be able to listen more attentively to me. I don't remember how often this occurred, but there were at least a few times when I felt cozy in the thought that I had God all to myself.

There was also a sense of God's nearness that stirred in me when I was in sacred places. Tinged as it might have been with some superstition or a child's imagination, I knew in some vague way that this or that church was God's house, and I thought it was good that God had colored windows (stained glass) and a special fragrance (possibly lingering incense or altar flowers). It was all very vague, and perhaps some psychologist with nothing better to do would analyze it in terms of religious programming. Somehow I know that it was not just this. God had touched me, and the first inklings of my own faith and the first desires for God were being formed in me.

I remember that, when the day of my First Holy Communion was approaching, I wrote the date on the back of my hand in indelible ink. Perhaps it was only a child's memo to himself, but I rather think that, even in those first days of faith, meeting God at one or another of God's points of rendezvous was something special to me.

ADOLESCENCE:
MOTIONS WITH MORE MEANING THAN I KNEW

During the forties, it was fairly common for a large part of the student body at a religious denominational high school to become "daily communicants," attending Mass and receiving the Eucharist every morning. I did this in my high school years for motives I cannot fully recall. But I did have some vague awareness that this was important, and my memory is stocked with a thousand images and remembered feelings of those early morning Masses, celebrated before school began each day.

Once I saw a sign promoting daily communion which read: "If you don't feel strong enough, maybe you're not eating the right kind of bread. Try the Bread of Life at the Testimonial Dinner in honor of Jesus Christ." I think it was due to my regular attendance at this banquet of Jesus that I was personally spared the usual moral agonies of adolescence. Out of my own experience I have become a staunch advocate of the Bread of Life and a firm believer in the reality of grace. It was not a case of preservation from taint in a high-walled, stained-glass world. Through most of my adolescence, I worked in the old Stock Yards in Chicago, carrying a switchblade knife for the emergencies of self-protection. Without much effort I resisted the frequent offer of a "reefer" and somehow was never ashamed to be a Christian, and a virginal Christian at that. I excelled in the boxing ring, and they called me "Battler." I also won quite a few medals for debating and oratory and was quite willing to argue for God, Church or Christian morality whenever and wherever they were challenged. I was an adolescent embattled and battling Christian, always ready and even eager for a little verbal infighting in defense of my faith.

VOCATION: "YOU HAVE NOT CHOSEN ME. I HAVE CHOSEN YOU."

It was also customary in the forties for seminaries to accept young men after high school. One day in my senior year I found myself across the desk from my spiritual counselor, and I heard myself telling him that I wanted to be a priest. Had you asked me then, as he did, why I wanted to become a priest, I would certainly have come up with some precocious reasons and motives. In fact, they would have been only convenient if articulate explanations of a deeper experience, the touch of God, the same current of grace that has moved me slowly but surely all the days of my life. Somehow entering the service of God as a priest seemed like the "right thing" to do. Everything else was mere verbiage (I was pretty good at that, too).

No one in my family or among my friends believed that I was serious about my intention to become a priest. Even my father, who was sure that I was destined to become a great lawyer, registered disbelief as the days dwindled down before my actual departure. I think I rather liked the idea that people wouldn't believe me. I didn't want to seem a pious, "destined-for-the-ministry-from-early-youth" type. I was the "Battler," the debater, the jazz-pianist, the jitterbug dancer. But the irresistible force of God's love and the current of God's grace was moving me to do a far better thing and taking me to a far better place.

SEEDS OF A CRISIS

The day before my departure for the seminary, I went across the street to say "goodbye" to the friendly neighbor who had bought roller skates and other gifts for the children in my family in those early days when we were poor and couldn't afford much. The old gentleman thought I was simply going away to college, but when it became clear that I was really going to a seminary to dedicate my

life and talents to God, he was suddenly and visibly distressed. He obviously regretted my decision. He warned me that I would be pouring my life and talents down a useless drain. "You see," he said, "there is no God."

He was a good man, and like many good men, he could not see how God could preside over a world in which there is war and suffering and evil. I said a polite, if embarrassed, goodbye and left him without ever once dreaming that he could possibly be right.

Then D-day and the Jesuit Novitiate. When I tell my students of today about the conditions of life in a Jesuit Novitiate of the forties, there is a definite credibility gap. I won't invite you to the test, but I assure you that in many ways, from the 5 a.m. rising, to the furniture that was early American orange-crate, the conversation of daily business in Latin, the long silences, and the four hours of prayer each day—it was a clear case of trauma for most of us.

THE FIRST STORMS OF DOUBT

When the novelty of the challenge wore off and the cost of this kind of discipleship became obvious, doubt struck me like a sudden crack of thunder on a summer's night, and the storm of uncertainty that followed darkened every area of my soul and life. Was there really a God? Was Jesus Christ really the Son of God? Is the Gospel fact or fiction? I ran in panic to prayer, but no one was there to meet me. The experience of God was for me one of a vast aloneness and barren silence: the death of all that had been with no vision or promise of a new birth. It was then that my old neighbor's words came back to me, with a new urgency and insistence. "You see, there is no God . . . there is no God . . . there is no God!"

I looked out at the stark surroundings and went through the motions of this spartan novitiate life sadly. In fact there was a constant funeral going on in my heart. God had left me—alone and here in this lonely place. The Master of Novices, who was supposed to guide us through this wilderness,

15

did not seem too alarmed at my sudden atheism. He counseled patience, with myself and with God. I thought he had not really gotten the full impact of my problem; he had not felt my whole world shaking.

This "dark night" of disbelief lasted four bleak and barren months. Then it happened. It was the beginning of the rest of my life, the pivotal religious experience of my own personal history. In the evenings, we novices had a fifteen-minute examination of conscience, during which we knelt on wooden blocks, our hands resting on our desks, our minds combing through the day for failures of commission and omission in thought, word, and deed. The only thing I did well, or at least so it seemed to me, was to get that wooden block in the right place. A well-adjusted kneeler, I used to say humorously to myself, was half the battle.

"HE TOUCHED ME!"

It happened on a definite Friday evening in the early spring, while I was kicking that kneeler into

place for the evening examination of conscience. With all the suddenness and jolt of a heart attack, I was filled with an experiential awareness of the presence of God within me. It has been said that no one can convey an experience to another but can offer only reflections on the experience. I am sure that this is true. I can only say, in trying to share my experience with you, that I felt like a balloon being blown up with the pure pleasure of God's loving presence, even to the point of discomfort and doubt that I could hold any more of this sudden ecstasy.

I think of the song "He Touched Me!," sung by Barbra Streisand, as the most apt way to describe the experience of that night. I am convinced that all human experiences, but especially the experience of an infinite God, are fundamentally incommunicable. Somehow God will always exceed the peripheries of human understanding. Precisely because God is infinite, God can never be brought into the focus of a finite human mind; and somehow these brushes with God's infinity cannot be fitted into finite concept or words. I can only tell you that God touched me.

If there is a "honeymoon" period in one's relationship with God, mine was the following year. There were repeated "touches," always at an unexpected time, always startling, and always incredibly warming. During this year I read for the first time Gerard Manley Hopkins' poem "The Wreck of the Deutschland," and found a poet's words to say what I was experiencing:

> Thou mastering me
> God! giver of breath and bread;
> World's strand, sway of the sea;
> Lord of living and dead;
> Thou hast bound bones and veins in
> me, fastened me flesh,
> And after it almost unmade, what with
> dread,
> Thy doing: and dost thou touch me
> afresh?
> Over again I feel thy finger
> and find thee.

"Over again I feel thy finger and find thee." I remember thinking that the touch of God excited a whole new vision and perception of life. It was like putting on badly needed glasses for the first time. A whole new and very beautiful world comes into view, and this new way of seeing things somehow diminishes the importance of every previous vision. Faith is indeed a new pair of inner eyes that see what was not seen before.

When God would come to me and touch me during this first year, I felt like Peter on Mt. Tabor, falling on his face before the smallest glimpse of God's beauty. Like Peter, I wanted to build tents high up in the mountain of God. I wanted to stop all the clocks and calendars of the world, to crystallize that moment of time. It was more than I could have ever dreamed in all my technicolor dreams.

TURN, TURN: A TIME TO ENDURE

I cannot be sure of the next part of my story. I do not know if Jesus simply led me, as He once did Peter, James and John, down from Tabor, from warmth and beauty into coldness and greyness. Or were the cold and greyness of my own making?

Fidelity is such a delicate and complex matter. Perhaps my own surrender to grace was far more pale and premature than I had realized. In any case, the lights of my warm new world gradually went out and a new wintertime set in.

One thing seemed permanently different in me. Having tasted the delights of God, I knew I could never return to earthly pleasures, to seek from them some compensation in my loneliness. I could not find God, but I knew that nothing and no one else would ever really satisfy me.

One summer's night during this period of trial, I was sitting at my desk studying when a moth came thumping at the screen of my window, trying to reach the light that burned on my desk. Again and again he would streak for the light and thump into the screen, drop down, circle around and try again. It struck me that he and his frustration symbolized my pursuit of God. For me there was some kind of mysterious veil over the face and heart of God. All the old warmth and comfort of God's presence were gone. Was I unfaithful, or was God asking my faith

to grow deeper roots? There is an admitted tendency in all of us to seek the consolations of God rather than the God of consolations. Perhaps this was the laboratory of life and love in which I was being asked to mature and be purified.

Paul Tillich once wrote that the death-resurrection cycle of Christianity is characteristic of growth in faith also. The old faith must die, eaten away by doubts, but only so that a new and deeper faith may be born.

Inroads of a Delusion: Something More Than God

However, I must be honest enough to admit that a delusion was entering my life at this time. Good people—and I trust that I am basically a good person—are rarely deceived by an obvious delusion. The devil never asks that the first step be a big one. During these seminary years, and especially in a religious order which prepares its men for careers in teaching, the visible emphasis is on brains. Theoretically and privately we were all trying to become saints; that is what we said and meant when we were on our knees. But sanctity is so difficult to measure and recognize. Only God reads the depths of the human heart, knows the reserves of faith and love found there. While several hours of the day were devoted to private or liturgical prayer, the bulk of the day during those years of study was given to learning.

Somehow in the labyrinths of my own psychological history, I was obviously programmed to be a competitor, always striving to be first, to be a winner. I jokingly admit that I would not let my grandmother beat me at a friendly game of checkers. Slowly but surely I found all the competitive energies and instincts inside me uncoiling as I entered the intellectual arena of seminary studies. It is my honest, retrospective judgment that at this point I was beginning to seek, to want something more than God. And this is my idea and definition of delusion. I was confusing the less important with the more important; I was confusing the means with the end. Instead of preparing myself intellectually to help build the Kingdom of God, I was grasping for the success that would sustain my ego. I was competing for the identity or image of a "very bright" student.

Jesus said: "Seek first the Kingdom of God and all these other things will be added unto you." He praised the "single eye" that seeks first and above all the glory of God. He told us of the "pearl of great price" that the heart should treasure; for where the treasure is, there the heart will be found too. I knew it all by heart, but not in my heart.

This is not to say that I did not pray during the years of my studies. I was deluded in, not divorced from, my search for God. However, very often my attempts at prayer were mere motion, going through the external gestures and assuming the external postures. But all of my heart was not there. My heart was a divided city. The tenacious desire to be a success as a student and as a teacher had seduced part of me, doubled my vision, divided my heart. These were, I fear, years of compromise; and a compromised seeker does not find the face or heart of God.

In My Weakness,
God's Strength and Patience

I cannot exonerate, nor can I excoriate myself for the mistakes of these years. The only real mistake is one from which we learn nothing, and I think I have learned much. But it is also true that to learn we must try to understand. How did it happen? Why did it happen? When did I become a fraction? Is this the human condition to which St. Paul referred when he declared that there "is another law warring in my members"? I think that we must be patient with ourselves, just as God is infinitely patient with us.

The identity or recognition which humans seek depends very much on "feedback." If we are praised for athletic talents, we tend to think of ourselves as athletes. If we are noticed for our good looks, we tend to identify with our physical appearance. In the years of my own neglect, all the feedback concerned performance in the classroom. The quick answers I gave, the perceptive questions I asked, the brilliant papers I wrote, the interesting classes I taught. These were the yardsticks by which others seemed to be measuring me, and the competitive demon in me anxiously sought their approval and applause.

The most serious aspect of delusions is that they tend to be habit forming, and the habits formed in youth can become tyrants in old age. I recall one night while I was in the seminary, waiting in the corridor of our infirmary while the Brother Infirmarian was tucking two bed-ridden priests in for the night. One of them was bitter and complaining, completely ungrateful. The other thanked the Brother and told him he would say an extra prayer for him before falling asleep. A sudden intuition gripped and frightened me. One day I would be one of those two priests: selfish and cantankerous or loving and grateful. But I knew, as I stood in the corridor of the infirmary, that the decision would not be made in the twilight of my life. It would be made in the young, formative years. It was being made then. Our yesterdays lie heavily upon our todays, and our todays lie heavily upon our tomorrows.

Ordination:
I Wanted to Come Running, But . . .

So I came to the altar of my ordination as a priest, with my habits, my internal cleavage, my ambiguous identity. On the day of ordination, I gave God a fraction of myself—how large or small I do not know. I did not feel very deeply the shame of my condition because I had never faced it honestly. The coping devices of human nature are ingenious. Vision and memory are highly selective. We tend to see and hear only what we want to see and hear. Having made a public holocaust of myself for God, I could not face the private fact that I was poking in the embers for unburned pieces. My lip-service was not my life-style. I talked a much better game than I was able to live.

The sun was bright and hot on the day of my ordination. The families and friends of the ordinands were crowded into our humid chapel, and we priests-to-be prostrated before the high altar at the beginning of the ceremony. This prostration is a gesture by which the priest-to-be signifies his dying, his dying to himself and to his own self-interest and advantage. He arises at the call of the Bishop, and his rising symbolizes that he is alive only to Christ and his Kingdom. His priesthood is interpreted theologically as a deeper identity with Christ. He is called, in fact, an *alter Christus,* an "other Christ." I have since agonized over the discrepancy between the word and gesture level of my life and the bone marrow of my commitment; but I did not do so then. The sun shone brightly; the ceremony was solemn and impressive, and I became a priest. My mother cried and hugged me proudly.

Old Delusions Do Not Die . . . At Least Not Quickly

After ordination, I concluded my studies and gained a doctorate degree in Europe. Europe was exciting. I learned three more languages and traveled as much as I could. But the heart of the matter was where it had always been. The doctoral work and degree were a contest, a competition, a win-lose sort of thing. And I was not about to lose. Was it my need for incense or that old force of habit?

With an accolade of *magna cum laude* embroidering my degree, I came back to the United States to teach in the seminary which I had attended. For the next five years, things remained pretty much the same. The pan-scales of success and failure were carefully supervised. Only success would do. I could not afford to be Avis. I had to be Hertz. Always number one. In the same mind, heart and life there was somehow coexisting a good, decent and compassionate man who wanted to serve God and the People of God. He went through the routine motions of prayer rather regularly, he studied and meditated on the Scriptures, and he answered most of the calls of those who needed him. Nothing he did was all evil, nor was it all good. Neither egotism nor altruism had won an uncontested victory in him.

Success, Ah Sweet Success . . .
But Then What?

The direction of my life at this time, I fear, was downhill. I became rather well known as a speaker and got a lot of mileage out of my mouth. I even gave stirring lectures and sermons on prayer. I think I was, in reality, substituting talk about prayer for actual performance. I became a successful teacher, a successful author, a successful speaker. The aroma of incense filled the air of my personal world. But inside me the crisis of being over thirty-five and needing a new and deeper meaning in life was forming like dark storm clouds. So you proved you could do it. Then you proved it again and again and again. Now where do you go? What do you do for an encore? What's it all about, Alfie? People take it for granted that you're going to be good, in the classroom, from the pulpit, on the lecture circuit.

I can clearly recall being introduced to audiences in such glowing terms that I was wincing inside, uncomfortable with the thought that I had better be good after that introduction. People expected it. It also seemed increasingly unbearable for me to have so many people demanding parts of me, making serious demands on my time, my energies, and my privacy. Someone once said that a priest is to the People of God what the town pump is to a village, a public utility that is there for all to use. I felt very "used," and the old clichés of gratitude and praise were getting tiresome, less needed and less consoling.

Where all this was leading and where I would have ended up is hard to say. Compromise has a way of extending and expanding itself. But the question is purely speculative now because the ever-patient, ever-merciful Lord of human history entered the history of my life again in two very decisive ways. "Over again I feel thy finger and find thee." I was re-routed, or, if there are many conversions in a human life, I was converted, profoundly changed by two experiences.

A Short Week With Long Consequences

A friend invited me to make a weeklong communications workshop and gave me a brochure which promised that this workshop would "put the participants in touch with their emotions." I remember my reaction. What? I smugly reassured myself that I was definitely in touch with my feelings and by a vote of one to nothing agreed that I had no need of such a workshop. Finally, after further insistence from my friend, I agreed to go "just to see what they're doing at these things." The result was a Copernican revolution that turned me inside out and upside down.

Somehow in sifting out the effects of that week, I became painfully aware that I had been lying to myself about me, about my feelings, my motives and goals. I had been so busy telling my feelings what they should be that I refused to let them tell me what they actually were. And I was so pre-occupied socially with being a good and holy priest that I denied people my own authenticity. I had been playing the role of priest, spinning out like a phonograph record the messages that had been recorded and drilled into me by those who trained me. I never told people how I really felt. I never even told myself.

I cannot stop here to elaborate on this turning point in my life. It would, as they say, require a book. I am happy to insert that this book has been written. I felt that I had to share my experience with others, and so I did write a book which I have called: *Why Am I Afraid to Tell You Who I Am?* (Thomas More Publishing, Allen, TX) I have been astounded by its success. No doubt many other people have the same kind of need I did to accept their emotions candidly and express them honestly. The reason I am inserting this whole experience here, however, is that it did profoundly affect my prayer life. What I have been trying to learn and practice about emotional self-awareness is very essential to my present way of praying. I hope to explain this more fully a little later on.

THE WEAK THINGS OF THE WORLD TO CONFOUND THE STRONG

While I was learning to put these lessons of self-awareness into practice, God brought me to the second turning point in my life at this time. I had been counseling a highly neurotic woman for several years. My "keen diagnostic eye" predicted that she would be a long-range effort and in the end would most likely be only a bit more comfortable and functional than in the beginning. Being programmed to success and in need of immediate reassurances, I find this type of person most difficult. Results always seem so slow in coming and so dubious when they do come. In the long and sometimes painful hours spent with this woman, one thing became very apparent to me. My desires to love and serve the People of God would be purified in this contact. I never dreamed that the God who writes straight with crooked lines would use this person as a major channel of grace to me.

In the several years that I was counseling this lady, the downhill trajectory of my own prayer-life continued. I am both amused and ashamed at the difference between the good game I was talking and the poor game I was living. The discrepancies in such a life are as painful as double vision. You see two things, and after a while you begin to wonder which one is real, or if anything is real. In my effort to be honest about my feelings and person, I was beginning to realize this, although I am sure that I forestalled ultimate realization of my condition of compromise because I knew this realization would make demands on me, would constitute a costly discipleship.

At any rate, my neurotic friend was weaving into and out of my life at the time. We talked at the beginning of the summer some six or seven years ago. There was the same old neurotic whine, the same indecision, the same egocentricity that is born of deeply embedded pain. I recall my unexpressed observation at the early summer conference that she had not become one bit more comfortable or functional than when we had first met. I was a failure, and, since I dread being a failure, I felt angry and disgusted.

WHO IS THIS THAT HE CURES THE SICK?

At the end of that summer, just before our university classes were to begin, I answered the phone to hear the voice of my troubled friend. I knew she would want another appointment and that I would agonize along with her while she resurrected the same old problems, like different verses of the same interminable song. But ah! The Spirit loves to surprise us. The voice I heard on the phone was somehow the same, somehow different. My "keen diagnostic ear" said that there was a new peace in her. I had to ask several times, "Who is this?" She quietly and peacefully said that she did not want an appointment, that she knew I was busy and wanted to take no more of my time. The only purpose of her call, she said, was to thank me for my patience and the help I had given over the last three years.

I couldn't believe what I was hearing. There was all the resonance of sincerity, but such abrupt personality changes just do not happen in real life.

So I said: "You're different, aren't you?" And she replied: "Oh, yes!"

"What happened?"

"I met Jesus Christ."

"You what?"

"I met Jesus Christ. Before this I knew about Him, but now I know Him."

"If you tell me that you have had a vision . . . "

"No, no vision. But I did meet Jesus Christ."

"I don't know whether you want to see me or not," I replied, "but I want to see you."

When she came to my office, my eye confirmed what my ear had led me to suspect. This was a "healed" person. I do not mean to detract one iota from the contribution they make to the lives of wounded human beings, but clinical psychology and psychiatry must not be allowed to pose as saviors or redeemers. Therapy can never be a substitute for a life of faith. I knew, from my training in psychology, that no reputable therapist could ever promise this kind of "cure," this new "wholeness." There is no plastic surgery to remove the psychological scars that all of us bear to some extent. By supportive psychotherapy we can be comforted, and by reconstructive psychotherapy we can be somewhat readjusted, develop new coping mechanisms, but . . . we cannot be healed or cured. This woman, seated before me, expressing gratitude and claiming to have met Jesus Christ, was "healed." She knew it, and I knew it.

Without any overtones of pride or egotism, she told me of her experience. She was invited to a prayer meeting. She told me how she decided to go, not really to pray, but to be able to say later that she had "tried everything, even prayer meetings." However, she was not prepared for the opening announcement of the leader of the prayer meeting. In large, oval tones, he began:

"We have come here tonight to pray, and if you can find it in your heart to join us, please stay. We both need and want you. But I have a feeling that some of you may have come out of curiosity, like spiritual Peeping Toms to see what goes on at prayer meetings. If this is why you came, and if you cannot find it in your heart to join us in reaching out to God, then I would like to ask you respectfully to leave."

O my God! Decision number one. She decided to stay, trying to pry her mind away from the "exit" sign, to turn it to the Lord. Then she heard one of the leaders of the group urge others to "open" to the Lord.

"Open all the doors and windows of your soul to the Lord. Don't keep any rooms locked or closed off to Him. Let Jesus take over. The depth of the faith that releases the power of God is measured by your willingness to let God direct your life. Raise yourself up to the Lord as a gift. Surrender your life and your heart to Him."

GOD'S HOUR—WATCH AND PRAY!

There is a theme in the New Testament about the "hour" of God in human history and in individual human lives. Watch and pray, Jesus urges us, because no one knows the day or the hour when the Lord will come. Having met Him in His many hours of intervention in my own life, I definitely believe this. And I am sure that my friend was experiencing one of God's hours with her own soul. She felt helpless to direct her own life successfully, and so, at the exhortation of one of the prayer group, she sincerely and almost desperately invited Jesus to come into her soul, her life, her world. She offered her unconditional surrender. He took her at her word, accepted her gift, became her Lord.

"For so many years," she told me, "there had been a high, hard, impenetrable wall between God and myself. I used to throw my little gifts over the wall and hope that someone was on the other side receiving them. It was impersonal, unsatisfying. But I thought it was the best I could do or even hope for.

"Somehow, in that moment—perhaps it was due to all the other people in the group praying for one another— the wall came down! Somehow Jesus was standing there with arms held out to embrace me. I knew Jesus as real for the first time."

While my friend continued to describe her moment of grace, God was somehow, strangely, having another "hour" with and in me. I was remembering hungrily all the things that had somehow slipped out of my hands, out of my life. I was remembering the night when I was moving that kneeler into place, the night God turned my world upside down, the night God "touched" me.

After my friend and I had talked in the afternoon, I asked her to return that night to join a group of university students who were to meet with me. She was happy to come, and I was happy to see the effect she had on the students. At my request, she told them something of shared-prayer meetings and then, much to my surprise, invited all of us to try it.

To have refused would have been like being against Mother's Day, so we all closed our eyes, bowed our heads, and began to pray. Alternately we prayed out loud, presumably addressing God and being willing to let the others listen to our conversation with God. It was my first attempt at this kind of "group" or "public" praying, and I was ill at ease. I was also a little rusty.

At the end of the evening, one of the students who had been present said to me, "Do you know what we were doing? We were performing for one another. All except that one lady. She really knows Jesus Christ, doesn't she?"

"Yes," I said, "and do you know what? She just met Him."

"What?"

A Springtime for My Soul

In the days that followed, I began to pray with a new intensity. From the early morning shower till the darkened moments while waiting for sleep, I kept inviting Jesus into my house of many rooms. I kept reassuring Him that I was ready to admit my own bankruptcy, my own helplessness to direct my life, to find peace and joy. I constantly invited the Holy Spirit to take down my walls, to destroy the barricades that were so many years in the building. I asked the Spirit to free me from the ingrained habit of competition, from the insatiable hunger for success, from the need for incense and adulation.

What began to happen in me almost immediately can be compared only to springtime. It seemed as though I had been through a long, hard-frozen wintertime. My heart and soul had suffered all the barrenness, the nakedness of nature in winter. Now in this springtime of the Spirit, it seemed as though the veins of my soul were thawing, as though blood was beginning to course through my soul again. New foliage and new beauty began to appear in me and around me.

Once more I had the sensation of putting on a new pair of badly needed glasses and seeing all kinds of things that had been obscured. Without an active faith the world can seem very alien, threatening. Human life can seem like a contest of endurance, the survival of the fittest. In the vision of faith, the world becomes warm and friendly. It is God's world. Other people are not really menacing. They are, in fact, my brothers and sisters because God is our Father and Jesus is our brother!

Was all this that was happening in me really from God, or could it all be explained away by some very natural, psychological theory? I have always believed that, when God touches human beings, the experience will survive three tests: (1) The *time* test: People touched by God will never be the same again. Even if the change is not dramatic, the experience of God will leave a permanent mark. Overheated emotions or subconscious suggestions come and go. God's hour has a definitely observable perdurance. (2) The *reality* test: The souls which have been touched by God will not be drawn up into an other-worldly posture or into bowered ivory towers of private ecstasy but will be deepened in their awareness of the world around them. They will see with their new eyes the beauty of their world; they will hear its music and poetry and know that it is a beautiful world. But they will also find themselves in deeper contact with the sadness in the hearts of humankind. They will notice a new awareness of the reality of their total environment, a new aliveness. As old St. Irenaeus, in the second century, once said: "The glory of God is a person fully alive." The true touch of God results in a new and vital "Yes!" to life. (3) The *charity* test: The human being who has opened to God's touch will be made more God-like by reason of that contact. That person will become more loving. St. John says that God is love and that anyone who fails to love cannot have known God. The person who abides in God abides in love. The grandest, most glowing of all God's miraculous interventions will always be the production of a loving person, the transformation of a go-getter into a go-giver. Essentially, this is what the hours or touches of God are all about. This is what God is doing. The gift of love is the highest gift of the Spirit.

My own renewed experience of God in these later years, just as my first Novitiate experiences of divine intimacy many years before, has seemingly passed these three tests. I feel an inner peace and certainty that these experiences were really from God.

The time test. It has been seven years since my neurotic friend came to me newly healed and became an instrument in my own healing. The reality of those moments and experiences of my "second spring" has not washed away like stimulated emotions that ride high for a time on the crests of exuberance. The touch of God has been for me rather like the electric realization of being loved. Though it did have its meteoric moment, flashing brightly against a darkened sky, the afterglow was never lost. In the last analysis it is the person who has experienced God who is the best judge of the experience. Perhaps that person is the only judge. I know about all the desires repressed in the subconscious, about self-fulfilling wishes, about the power of autosuggestion. But I know with an imperturbable inner certainty that my loving God has touched me! In this whole matter of faith, it is God who takes and keeps the initiative. We move to the rhythms of God's grace, and we find God at the meeting place, and at the time God chooses.

The reality test. I found myself, as a result of the experiences I have described, in a deeper and more meaningful contact with the world about me. I am reminded of Dag Hammarskjold's remark that "on

the day I first believed, for the first time the world made sense and life had meaning." I have read that most theologians believe that the most serious obstacle to a life of faith is *inattention*. The world is charged with the presence and glory of God, but many do not see. We are too preoccupied with ourselves, too concerned about our own needs, too bent upon our own pleasures. Daily, I feel God moving me out of this lonely little insulated and isolated world with its population of one. God is more and more deeply inserting me into the human drama, putting a new "yes" to life into my heart and on my lips.

The charity test. I have written and given sermons on love and charity. I have been a man of many facile answers on the subject. But it was the old problem of talking a better game than I was living. There was a painful distance between the word-level and the life style of my existence. People were making irritating demands upon my time, bleeding me of my energies, leaving me less and less to call my own. I remember gazing at the telephone and thinking of it as an instrument of torture. It just kept ringing and those who called always had requests of one kind or another. A paranoid feeling of aloneness was growing inside me. I was developing a secret anger towards the rest of the clergy. I wondered what they were doing. Weren't there some other Messiahs around these days?

But, ah, the fault, dear Brutus, is not with our stars or the endless needs of humanity. The real rub is within ourselves. The basic question is: Do you really want to love? Are you willing to be the "public utility," the town pump which is there for all to use? Do you really want to let Jesus be reincarnated in your humanity? Jesus is the "man for others." If you give yourself to Him, He will immediately put you in the service of others in one way or another. Do you really want to volunteer for this life of loving? You can't do it on your own. He must do it in you. Will you have enough faith to release His power into your life? These are the only pertinent questions.

I am now deeply convinced that the power of love is from God. I believe that no one can truly love unless God is active within him or her. I hear Jesus say, "Without me you can do nothing. You can bear no fruit. I am the vine and you are the branches. Cut off from me you are dead." I hear St. John say that only the person who knows God can know the meaning of love. I hear St. Paul describe love as the highest and greatest gift of the Spirit. Wherever I have found love I have felt the presence of God, God at work in the minds and hearts and muscles of men and women.

My experience of God has been working this transformation in me, too. Oh, I am still a very selfish person. God is not finished with me yet. Others may not think of me as a very effective lover, but they do not know the before and after; they cannot read the motives of the heart. The process of divinization, in which God makes us more and more to God's image and likeness, is a slow, gradual, and often painful process. I am still a pilgrim. But I have been touched and I am partially transformed. This is the basis for my hope. The God who has touched me in the past will act again and again in my life. Over again I will feel God's finger and find God.

THE EFFECTS ON MY PRAYER:
SPEAKING TO GOD

Where has all this led me? Where has God, through all this, been leading me?

I now understand and approach prayer as *communication in a relationship of love*, a *speaking* and a *listening* in truth and in trust. Speaking to God honestly is the beginning of prayer; it locates a person before God. I believe that the primary "giving" of love is the giving of oneself through self-disclosure. Without such self-disclosure there is no real giving, for it is only in that moment when we are willing to put our true selves on the line, to be taken for better or for worse, to be accepted or to be rejected, that true interpersonal encounter begins. We do not begin to offer ourselves until we offer ourselves in this way, for love demands presence, not presents. All my gifts (presents) are mere motion until I have given my true self (presence) in honest self-revelation.

As in all interpersonal relationships, so in the relationship with God, I do not put myself into God's hands or confront the divine freedom of choice to accept me or reject me, to love me or to loathe me, until I have told God who I am. Only then can I ask: Will you have me? Will you let me be yours? Will you be mine? Martin Luther's first law of successful prayer is: *Don't lie to God!* In speaking to God in the dialogue of prayer, we must reveal our true and naked selves. We must tell God the truth of our thoughts, desires and feelings, whatever they may be. They may not be what I would like them to be, but they are not right or wrong, true or false. They are me.

When I began praying to God this way, exposing my raw and naked feelings, I knew why God had led me to make that communications workshop to which I have referred previously. I knew why God had taught me to locate my changing feelings and desires, enabling me to tell my truth to others. I am sure that this has benefited me in many other ways, but certainly it has enabled me to speak more honestly to my God. It has freed me from the lie of those prefabricated pious clichés that are death to true conversational prayer. I have told God where I really live, in belief and unbelief. I have told of my weariness in answering God's call, of my emotional resentment at being a public utility, a servant to be taken for granted. I have ventilated all my neurotic, throbbing emotions, never claiming to have *the* truth, but always willing to tell *my* truth .

I have been like Job of the Old Testament, cursing the day God made me, and like the prophet Jeremiah, accusing God of making not a prophet but a fool of me. I have been a King David singing of God's mercy and forgiveness, which I have always needed along the way of my pilgrimage.

There is something so healing about "letting it all hang out" with God. The psychiatrist Jung defined neurosis in terms of an inner cleavage, a war within, an existence of fractionhood, division. With Paul we all know that there is "another law warring in my members." The real problem is confronted when we come to the question of our willingness to accept ourselves in this human condition of weakness. Will we be comfortable as a fraction, a creature of ambiguity whose evil is always mixed somehow with good and whose good is always somehow tainted with evil?

I am sure that this comfort in the human condition depends for me on whether God will accept me this way or not. I feel that I am worth only what I am worth in God's eyes. All the rest is charade. So I have to put myself on the line the way I am. Charades with God is wasted time. I have to put myself in the posture of trusting God's greatness and understanding. This is the essential beginning of prayer.

LISTENING TO GOD

If speaking to God is no simple matter, my experience has convinced me that listening to God in the dialogue of prayer is even more difficult. How does God communicate to me? How does God disclose who God is after I have revealed myself? Do I have to wait hours, days, weeks or even years to see what God will do with and about my openness? Or is there a more immediate and direct response? I think that there is.

I ask myself questions like these: Can God put a new idea directly and immediately into my *mind?* Can God give me a new perspective in which to view my life with its successes and failures, agonies and ecstasies? Can God put new desires into my *heart,* new strength into my *will?* Can God touch and calm my turbulent *emotions?* Can God actually whisper words to the listening ears of my soul through the inner faculty of my *imagination?* Can God stimulate certain *memories* stored within the human brain at the time these memories are needed?

These questions all seem critical to me. If the answer to these questions is *yes,* then God has at least five channels through which grace can reach me, five antennae in my human anatomy through which God can "touch" me directly and immediately. If the answer to these questions is *yes,* then my present method of prayer makes

sense. If, however, the answer to these questions is *no*, then I have been badly deluded and I have nothing to offer you.

Of course I feel sure that God can and does reach us in these ways. I think of the whole Bible as simply a written record of such religious experience, of God invading human history and human lives, of God speaking to humankind. I also believe that this God is available and anxious to speak to you and me. Yes, just as anxious as God was to speak to Abraham, Isaac and Jacob, Isaiah and Jeremiah. I believe that God has spoken to others before me, that God's inspirations have resulted in many beautiful lives and deeds for God and all of humankind. I have always believed this, that God stopped Saul of Tarsus short on the road to Damascus, that God pursued the reluctant Augustine down the labyrinths of human weakness, that God inspired the founder of my own order, Ignatius of Loyola, to hang up his soldier's sword and to do battle only for the Kingdom of God. Oh yes, God did these great deeds in these great people.

But would God come to me? This was harder for me to grasp until I stopped asking the wrong question and began to ask the meaningful question. I had been asking: Who am I, O my God, that you would come to me in tenderness and intimacy? How could I ever be so important to you? What do I have to offer? I was trapped in my old preoccupation with self. The real question is, of course: Who are you, my God? Who are you that you would come to me and speak to me, that you would fill my poor finite mind with your thoughts and perspectives, that you would enable me to see this world through your eyes, that you would put your strength and desires into my frail will, that you would pour your divine grace into this vessel of clay? Who are you that you graciously accept the loaves and fish of my life to feed the hungry throughout the world? Who are you? Show me your face, fold me and my life into your loving arms, let me feel your fire and the soothing touch of your hand on the face of my thirsting soul.

I pray by telling God who I am and by listening as God reveals to me not only who God is, but also who I am, and what my life and this world mean to God. My listening is the silent turning over to God the five faculties or powers of perception through which I truly believe that God comes to me.

THE ANTENNAE OF MY LISTENING

My Mind. After putting myself before the Lord, God comes to me to help me see the person, the problems I have described through God's eyes and in the Lord's eternal perspective. God puts ideas into my mind, and especially perspectives. The Lord widens my vision, helps me to see what is really important in life and to distinguish the really important from the unimportant. I have always wanted to define *delusion* as the confusion of what is important in life with the unimportant. I personally get uptight, blow things up out of all proportion, especially when the lightning strikes close to the home of my ego. I enter the wrong arenas to do battle, focus on the wrong issues of contention. And I tell my God all about it. Then

God comes, and, in a gentle way, fills my mind with divine thoughts and God's vision.

My Will. The one thing I have learned about myself in the last forty years of life is that I am weak. No pretense or sham. No mock humility. I am truly a weak person, badly in need of redemption. In the days of my early fervor in the service of God after entering the seminary, I used to offer God my day upon awakening. I promised God a "perfect" day, a day of perfect love and service. In my night prayers. I could only offer the Lord my remorse. It has taken me a long time to sincerely distrust my own strength and to turn my life over to God.

Only when I was willing to admit my nothingness did God begin to make something of me. In my weakness God's strength is made manifest. But more than simply steeling my will to the chal- lenge of costly discipleship, God has come to me in prayer and put into my will new desires. Psy- chologically as well as spiritually, it seems so important that we be persons of desire. I am sure that every great accomplishment in all of human history began with the birth of a desire in some human heart.

So God comes to me, in the listening, receptive moments of prayer and transfuses power into me; God rekindles my desires to be God's person, to be a public utility, a town pump for the Kingdom of God, just as God's Son was during His life among us.

My Emotions. When I am emotionally embittered or discouraged, when I experience that dull ache of loneliness, or I am saddened in the trough of some criticism or failure, God comes to comfort me. It is as though God's healing power is extended to my neurotic feelings. If Jesus can make a leper clean, He can make a neurotic normal. Often I ask Jesus to raise the hand which calmed the winds and waves of Gennesareth over my turbulent soul. Make me calm and tranquil, too. However, I firmly believe that God comes not only to comfort the afflicted, but also to afflict the comfortable.

There are times when God comes not to trouble me, but only to rearrange my values or make me aware of someone in need; and always to challenge me to grow. I have never asked the Lord for a problemless life or a plastic tranquility. I ask only for that peace which knows what is important and what is unimportant, only for that serenity which knows that I have been loved and that I am called to love.

My Imagination. Somehow the same people who believe that God can enter the mind with divine ideas and perspectives, the will with divine strength and desires, or the emotions with divine peace, balk at the thought that God can stimulate the imagination to hear inwardly actual words or see actual visions. My own mother once told me, in a hushed and confidential way, that God has often spoken to her, giving her rather specific directives for her life. She said, "I wouldn't tell anyone else because others would certainly think I am a little crazy." I remember reassuring her that it runs in the family. For I, too, have heard God and perceived inwardly a gentle loving look of Jesus, and I believe that this was really the touch of God, stimulating my imagination.

This, of course, was the problem with Joan of Arc and her voices. The following is a short excerpt from George Bernard Shaw's play, *St. Joan:*

Robert: How do you mean? voices?

Joan: I hear voices telling me what to do. They come from God.

Robert: They come from your imagination.

Joan: Of course. That is how the messages of God come to us.

Granted that it might be difficult to distinguish words coming from the stimulus of God's grace from those which might proceed simply from self-stimulation or autosuggestion, the reality must not be denied simply because God's grace in us can be simulated. God has access to us through this power of imagination. I once discussed this avenue of God into us with a prayerful psychologist, and it was her opinion that there would always be "something surprising, distinctive and lasting" in the communication of God. I think she is right.

I remember once asking what God might wish to say to me, or ask of me. It was a moment of white-heat fervor, when I felt ready to hear anything. In the quiet moments of listening, inwardly I heard the words: "I love you." I felt disappointed. Oh, I knew this. But God came back to me, this time through the channel of my mind. Suddenly it became very clear to me that I had never really accepted and interiorized the love of God for me. In the flash of this graced intuition I saw that I had always known that God had been patient with me and forgiving; but it struck me that I had never really opened to the reality of God's love. The Lord was right, I slowly realized. I had never really heard the message of God's love. When God speaks, there will always be "something surprising, distinctive and lasting."

My Memory. The final channel or antenna of human reception to the communication of God is the memory. It is said that love consists in equal part of memory and intuition. We have also remarked that the only real mistake a person makes is the one from which he or she has learned nothing. When God communicates to us through the stimulation of some stored memory, God can stir up our love by reminding us of the divine tenderness and goodness in the past, thus fortifying us to meet the present moment and have hope for the future. God can also prevent us from repeating an old mistake by reminding us of the past. For me, at least, the bedrock of my faith and gratitude is the *remembered goodness* of God in the history of my life: the Lord's hours, the touches. "All I ask of you is forever to remember me as loving you."

THE NEED FOR "CONVERSATIONAL" PRAYER

What I want to say in italics is that through these channels we can regularly experience direct and immediate communication from God. It is admittedly difficult to listen delicately and perceptively to God. I am still learning how to do this. But I have had enough experience to sense the possibilities for the truly attentive and tuned-in person. I am personally sure that, when we learn to sit quietly at the feet of God and rest in God's loving presence, the Lord will in one or all of the above ways tell us who God is, who we are and what we are called to do and be for God and for one another.

There are other types of prayer, almost as varied as human experience itself. There is the prayer of finding God in natural beauty, in music, in dance, in interpersonal relationships. There is the prayer of meditation, the prayer of silence. But the kind of prayer in which God is my conversational partner, the prayer of mutual self-disclosure, is the staple of my own prayer life. I find and worship the Lord in nature, in music and poetry, in my brothers and sisters, in the lightning and thunder over my Sinais and in the burning bushes of Chicago. But I have a feeling that, if I did not come to know God in this prayer of conversation, I would not be attentive to the divine presence in these other places, especially in the soft, still whispers of the currents of grace that move almost imperceptibly around me.

We do not need a theologically accurate portrait of God to begin this dialogue of prayer. If this were the case, none of us could ever begin to pray.

Getting to know God is a dialogical process. We begin with mistaken impressions, distorted ideas, unfounded fears and personal prejudices. But gradually, as we unfold ourselves to God and God unfolds the divine presence to us, we correct old erroneous impressions, gain new insights, experience new facets of the mysterious and tender God who cannot forget us even if a mother should forget the child of her womb. Having been wrong about God doesn't mean that we haven't been talking to God. It is only by perseverance in this type of prayer that we will come to be less and less wrong about the Lord until that day when we shall know God even as we are known.

What I needed most, in arriving at this moment in my life, was the knowledge that God really wanted to be intimately close to me. I needed to be rid of the deistic concept of God as distant, uninterested, inoperative in me and in my human powers. But most of all, I needed some success in this method of prayer. I needed to feel the touch of God, to experience the thoughts of God stretching my mind, to feel the firmness of God's strength and desires in my will, to hear God's voice and experience light in the darkness of my nights, to feel calm in the moments of my distress. Only then, in these meanderings into the mercy of this tender, present, available God did I know that God really wanted me to belong and wanted to be the portion of my heart forever. Only then, with this success, did I know that God could never seem the same and I could never be the same again.

Conclusion: Two Short Stories

I would like to conclude this story of my own pilgrimage with two brief stories about my own experiences with this prayer of dialogue. The first has to do with the cigarette habit. I had acquired the habit early. Experimentation began when I was eight years old, although official acquisition of the habit was delayed by parental decree and enforcement.

In the course of my struggles with the tyranny of nicotine, I enjoyed brief little victories. But there was always that weak moment when I promised myself it would be "just one," and I was back in my old chains, a prisoner of my old habits. When medical evidence began to pile up, and lung cancer, heart trouble, emphysema, and respiratory infections were linked rather conclusively to my tyrant, I tried again and again, but in the end my efforts were always unsuccessful. More and more I felt helpless and conquered, and this is for me— with my well-cultivated myth of self-sufficiency and strength—the most difficult of all admissions. On an even deeper level I had strong guilt feelings about my weakness.

One morning, while I was praying and dying to get to that first cup of coffee and cigarette, I had the feeling that God wanted me to talk about this matter. So I admitted my shame, and I remember ending with the painful admission that "I guess I just don't have the strength." Figuratively I threw myself on the mercy of God and crumbled there under the weight of my repeated failures at self-conquest.

Then I heard the words inside me: "I have the strength for you. It is yours if you ask for it."

"Okay," I said. "You give me your strength and you've got yourself a deal."

All I can tell you is that since that moment several years ago I have not smoked. As I remember, there were the so-called "nicotine fits" for a very short while, and then all inclination to smoke disappeared completely. What is even more mysterious to me is that God seems to have erased all memory of what it was like to smoke. St. Augustine's lament that memory is indeed a sad privilege had been obvious to me in all my previous efforts to quit smoking. The sad privilege of memory bothered me after every meal, whenever I saw someone else lighting up. All that is gone now, and I feel like a person who has never smoked. I think my present attitudes and freedom are comparable to those of the many members of Alcoholics Anonymous who know that they have won sobriety only through the strength of a power greater than themselves, only through the strength of God infused into them.

Months after it had become obvious that God had touched me again, had talked to me and braced my willpower with strength, I was listening to God in prayer, and I thought God was saying: "I have many other gifts to offer you much greater than the power to stop smoking. I have great gifts of the power to love, to be at peace, to find meaning in your daily life, to be truly joyful."

"Lay them on me," I replied. "All my lids are off. Pour all these graces into me."

I felt the soft smile of God's love. "No, not now. But when you have come to the point that you did in the matter of smoking, when you know that you cannot love with your own powers, that you can't provide your own peace, or find meaning in life with your own formulas, when you are sure that you can't be truly joyful until I give you my joy, when you know all these things—then I will give you these graces."

Apparently God will not aid and abet my human vanity or pride. The Lord will not encourage my myth of self-sufficiency. It all makes great sense to me, and I can see why pride is the root of all evil, and how my own stubborn pride even now limits the action of God in my life. I daily ask for the grace of true humility, to be willing to admit my nothingness so God can make something of me.

The final story of illustration happened just one year ago. I belong to a religious order, and our "Father Provincial" had appointed three theologians to visit the various local communities of our province and give a panel presentation on "Devotion to Jesus Today." The final presentation was to be made to the community of the university at which I teach, my community.

These were the men with whom I live and teach. I have given so many speeches in public I am rarely nervous. But this night I was definitely nervous. I thought I knew why. No prophet is honored in his own country, and all that. So, while the other two theologians on the panel were giving their presentations before mine, I was silently praying. I asked Jesus to raise His becalming hand over me. Pour your peace into me. Help me to relax and do well.

Nothing happened. I mean nothing. Now I am a great believer that symptoms are really significant messages. A headache is telling me something, that I am under some tension, and that I will learn something about myself if I will trace the symptom to its cause. I never reach for an aspirin without asking my pain what it is trying to tell me. So I examined my nervousness, in consultation with the divine physician, Jesus. I heard His diagnosis, and the words I heard inside me that night have had a profound effect upon me and upon my life. He said:

"You are nervous because you are getting ready to give a performance. You want to impress your brothers, to make sure they realize what a 'gem' they have in you. I don't want a performance. I want an act of love. Your brothers do not need you to impress them, but to love them."

In this communication, Jesus reached very deeply into my life. I suddenly and clearly realized that much of my life has been performance, performance geared to impress people. I managed to keep the butterflies of nervousness in control most of the time, but this kind of personal, egotistical ambition is a Shylock which demands its pound of human flesh. The parasites of an egocentric life drain off so much human energy and destroy so much human peace.

I once read that the singer-actress Mary Martin would stand in the wings of the stage before her performances and would hold out her arms in the direction of her audience, repeating: "I love you. I love you. I love you." Then, on cue, she would go out to act and sing for those she loved, feeling very much at home because it was an act of love.

On the night of my presentation to my community, I made a silent act of love, and then I spoke to my brothers whom I love. I wanted to tell them at the end: I don't know if I have informed you or even helped you, but, my Brothers, I have in this moment loved you!

I would like to say this to you, too, dear Reader. I am not sure what my story has been worth to you. It may well be that you are far advanced in the dialogue of prayer and well beyond me. Some of the admissions I have made in these pages, especially those concerning my own weakness and infidelity, came hard for me, and the thought of making them public in print causes a little tightening inside me. But I want to do it for you. The real gift of love is self-disclosure. Until we have given that, we have given nothing. And I hope that you will accept this gift as I have intended it: as an act of love. May God bless you.

John Powell, S. J., Loyola University,
Chicago, Illinois, 1974

EPILOGUE

This little book was written over twenty years ago. No one is more astonished by its lasting popularity than I am. The title has been changed from *He Touched Me* to *Touched By God*. This change was made as an effort to practice "inclusive language."

In the year before it was born, I remember getting a letter from Maxie Dunnam. He was at the time the editor of *The Upper Room*. He told me of his plans to edit a series of booklets on prayer. He added that he didn't want a book on the theory, but on the personal experience of prayer. So I sat down to tell my story, the story of my own experience with prayer. I called it *He Touched Me: My Pilgrimage of Prayer.* After Maxie had received the manuscript of the booklet, he called me on the phone. In a delightful southern accent, he said: "Oh, John, this deserves a wider circulation than we can give it." He suggested that Argus Communications do a dual publication. Dick Leach, the owner of Argus, was happy to do this.

It is strange that while this book has not been as widely popular as some of the others, it has brought in more correspondence than any other. It must have struck some chord, caused some recognition in the experience of others.

Since the book was first published, there have been new joys and new personal trials and purifications. At present I am having some difficulty with the added fragility of "growing old." I feel like a young man trapped in an old man's body. God has over the years turned on the lights frequently. But God has just as frequently turned them off. My personal world has been flooded with light, and also at other times seemed dark and lonely.

Several years ago I went back to the scene of my first transforming encounter with God. I remember talking to the trees. They saw me entering the Novitiate when I was a seventeen-year-old boy. They heard my voice and laughter. They recorded my hidden tears and loneliness. It was nostalgic, to say the least.

As I turn the pages of the album of my past life, I have a growing certainty of this: God is working out a plan in my life. Sometimes it is very comforting. I sit in God's lap. At other times God leaves me painfully clinging by my fingernails to faith. Perhaps this is the purest kind of faith. It has been said that the hour of God comes at the limit of our endurance. I keep remembering John Banister Tabb's verse about "God's Weaving." God sees our lives from the topside. God alone knows what the weaving looks like.

> My life is but a weaving
> Between my Lord and me.
> I cannot choose the colors
> He works steadily.

Often he weaves sorrow
And I in foolish pride
Forget that he sees the upper
And I the lower side.
The dark threads are as needful
In the weaver's skillful hand
As the threads of gold and silver
In the pattern God has planned.

The big question most of us wrestle with is this: Does prayer change anything? My answer is: Oh yes, it changes us. And this is what is most important. I, we, do not have the simple faith that can come only through prayer, if we do not go to God as little children, God cannot confirm our prayer with Divine Presence, Power and Peace. Only when we realize that all our blessings do come from God, who is our Mother and Father, then only can God bless us abundantly. God can confirm us only in truth.

One of the letters that the original book brought to me was that of a young woman, who was determined to commit suicide. She had led what she described as a "bad life." The only way to end this misery was suicide. It had to be suicide by drowning. She had fantasized the ocean as a great watery mother, who would rock her forever in the arms of her waves. When she arrived at the ocean beach, early in the morning, she was alone. But the sea was no mother. It was a snarling beast, hissing restlessly.

The young woman continued: "So I walked along the sandy rim of the ocean, reasoning that even if I had to be destroyed by this hissing beast, death was my only choice. Die I must." Then came a mysterious voice, very loud and clear, though no one else was on the beach. The voice commanded the young woman to "Stop. Turn around and look down." She did this only to discover that the ocean had come in over her footprints. When its waves washed back, her footprints were gone.

The voice continued, now tenderly: "Just as you see the waves of the ocean erasing your footprints, so has my love and mercy erased your past. I am calling you to live and to love, not to die."

The letter to me went on: "So I turned away from the ocean. I have found a good and happy life. But

I have told no one of the experience at the ocean, for two reasons: First, it was a very personal experience and consequently not easy to share. But secondly, I have told no one for fear of laughter. I don't want others to throw back their heads and say: 'Oh, you didn't want to die so you made up a voice to console yourself, to talk yourself out of it.'

"So, just as you concluded your book with: 'This is my act of love for you,' so is this my act of love to you. Please take it in gentle hands."

I have appreciated that letter, not only at the time I received it, but over the years since. My reflection and reaction is this. We are all pilgrims on our way to God's House, and during the course of our lives, God periodically touches each of us. I pray that I will be sensitive enough to perceive this touch, and to know that God is calling me to live and to love. "Watch and pray," says the Lord Jesus, "for you do not know when the hour of God will come to you."

Remember me as loving you.

John Powell, S.J.

OTHER BOOKS BY JOHN POWELL

Solving the Riddle of Self
Simple enough question: Who are you? But so few us ever take the time to be guided on a journey of true self-discovery. Now John Powell focuses on this most central question in his NEW BOOK!

A Life-Giving Vision
(How to Be a Christian in Today's World)
"Summarizes all the important things I have ever written"—John Powell. 352 pages with four-color original art, this is a great Powell gift idea!

Why Am I Afraid to Tell You Who I Am?
This extraordinary book, which has changed countless lives, takes a straightforward approach to helping people grow in self-awareness, self-esteem, and inter-personal communication skills.

Why Am I Afraid to Love?
Tear down the walls that you've built to protect yourself from rejection. That's the urgent message in this classic book on the universal human desire to love and to be loved.

The Secret of Staying in Love
Communication is the secret! The author lays out practical ways to build love, open lines of communication, and share feelings openly and honestly.

Fully Human, Fully Alive
Where do true health and happiness begin? John Powell believes they begin with positive attitudes about ourselves, others and God. The rewarding results will be

new self-confidence, healed relationships, an increased ability to pray, a pleasing new capacity for enjoyment, and heightened sensitivity to others' needs and feelings.

Happiness Is an Inside Job

Like the elusive butterfly, happiness can't be directly pursued. Instead, happiness is attained by doing something else—and that something else is the content of this exceptional book. The author details a clear and effective process called the "happiness habit," which involves practicing ten life tasks that lead to peace, satisfaction and happiness.

Will the Real Me Please Stand Up?

This powerful study in human growth explores communication as the lifeblood of every human relationship. Twenty-five basic principles of communication are explained in this best-seller.

Unconditional Love

No one writes about love in quite the way that John Powell does! Citing human love as the energizing force behind all real living, he extols unconditional love as a permanent gift of the heart and the only love worthy of the name.

The John Powell Collection

Seven of John Powell's perennial best-sellers—with more than 10 million copies sold—are now more vital, appealing and readable than ever! All seven titles are packed in a handsome new slipcase, making the John Powell Collection a perfect gift for any time of the year.

TO ORDER CALL TOLL FREE
(800) 264-0368